# Why Do THEY Do That?

written by
Sandy Sotzen, M. Ed.

illustrated by
Catherine Suvorova.

To Ryan – thanks for helping me carry the weight of Autism; like the chicken, I know it wasn't light.

To Tyler – I will forever be your voice; I've got you buddy.

S.S.

No part of this publication may be reproduced in whole or in part, stored in a retrieval system, or transmitted in any form or by any means, electronic, mechanical, photocopying, recording, or otherwise, without prior written permission of the publisher. For information regarding permission, write to the publisher, Storybook Genius, at: 220 Jefferson Street, Washington, Missouri 63090 or visit them at www.sbgpublishing.com  ISBN 978-1-952954-52-8 Text copyright© 2021 by Sandy Sotzen. Illustrations copyright© 2021 by Sandy Sotzen.

All rights reserved. Published by Storybook Genius, LLC.

Samantha asks her mom many questions each day!
And each day, her mom smiles and patiently responds to each and every question!

One summer day while standing by the fountain in the park, Samantha noticed a boy jumping up and down and moving his hands up and down very quickly. It reminded Samantha of a baby bird flapping its wings.

Samantha quietly whispered to her mom, "Mama, why does he do that?"

"Samantha, the boy is excited about the water. He may have a disability called Autism that can make it hard for him to communicate his feelings. So he might jump, flap, or spin around to communicate and calm himself down," explained Mom.

Samantha tried flapping her hands to see how it felt.

It felt good to her and it made her feel calm, too!

As they headed for the playground equipment at the park, Samantha noticed another girl about her age wearing a bright pink helmet. She was not riding a skateboard or bike.

"Mama," asked Samantha, "Why is she wearing that?"

"The little girl might have a seizure disorder that could make her fall to the ground and hit her head. The helmet protects her. Go over, introduce yourself, and ask her if she'd like to play," said Mom.

Samantha ran over to the girl and they spent the rest of the day playing together!

When Samantha got home she decided that she wanted to dig her helmet out of her toy box!

For dinner, Samantha and her mom went to their favorite restaurant! Samantha noticed a boy sitting at the next table using a tablet to tell his mom what he wanted to eat. He tapped several buttons and a computer voice quietly said, "I want a cheeseburger, fries, and soda." His mom nodded her head, smiled, and then told the person taking orders what he wanted to order.

"Mama, why did that boy use that device to order his dinner?"

"Samantha, he may be unable to speak but can make choices. The device allows him to choose what he wants and then it does the speaking for him," explained Mom.

Samantha spent the rest of the night trying to sound like the boy's device to her kittens.

On Saturday, Samantha and her parents went to a carnival at her school. She was surprised at how crowded the gym was with people, games, and food booths!

While waiting in line for tickets, Samantha noticed that the little girl in front of her was wearing bright yellow headphones over her ears and she was making a humming sound.

Samantha asked her mom, "Mama, why does she do that?"

Her mom helped her understand that the little girl was wearing headphones and making humming sounds to block out some of the noise. She explained that some children are sensitive to loud noises and they can make them feel uncomfortable. Samantha wished she had her dad's big black headphones to wear while she was in the noisy gym!

Later in the week, Samantha and her mom went to the airport to pick her dad up from a business trip. Samantha loved airports! While she was waiting, Samantha was thrilled to see a beautiful black dog wearing a red vest walking beside a teenager. The teenager had a cane she was tapping on the ground with her right hand. And she held the dog's harness with her left hand.

It wasn't long before Samantha asked,
"Mama, why does she do that?"

Samantha's mom explained that the girl was blind and the dog and the cane helped her get through the airport without bumping into things. She also told Samantha to never pet a service dog while it's working or helping its owner. Samantha took her umbrella and tapped around the airport until she saw her dad and ran to give him a hug!

For the rest of the summer, Samantha's mom continued to talk with her about children who were **differently abled**, not disabled, and how she should be a good friend and a good listener, no matter how they were communicating with her. Samantha promised that she'd do that!

A new boy moved into the neighborhood that summer. He was hearing impaired. Samantha and her mom checked out a book on sign language at the library so Samantha could welcome him with sign language.

Samantha thought it was fun to use her fingers to say things instead of words and she was very excited to have a new friend!

By the end of summer, Samantha's feet had grown, so her mom took her to buy new shoes! Samantha was trying on a new pair when she heard a great deal of screaming and crying coming from a boy in front of her. Samantha grabbed her mom's hand as she watched the boy cry and hit himself over and over again. Normally, Samantha would have been very sad for the boy (and a bit scared), but instead she remembered all that her mom had told her about kids who are **differently abled**.

"Mom, I have an idea," she whispered to her mom.

Samantha knelt down near the boy and she opened her box of fish crackers. Samantha's mom asked the little boy's mother if they could help. Both the little boy's mother and Samantha's mother knelt by the little boy and whispered to him and rubbed his back. In about ten minutes, the boy began to calm down and was no longer kicking, screaming, or hurting himself.

Then Samantha offered the little boy a goldfish.
He took one and smiled at her.
Samantha smiled back.
It felt good that she could help the little boy feel better.

That night before bed, Samantha's mother tried to explain that the little boy was not being bad but that he just needed extra help to calm down.

CPSIA information can be obtained
at www.ICGtesting.com
Printed in the USA
LVHW051102301021
701903LV00005B/47